DATE DUE		
OCT 1 9 2001		
AUG 0 5 2003		
AUG 2 4 2004		
MAR 1 6 2006		
NOV 15 2006		
AUG 2 4 2009		

Emergency Vehicles

by Dayna Wolhart

Published By
Capstone Press, Inc.
Mankato, Minnesota USA

Distributed By

◖P CHILDRENS PRESS®

CHICAGO

CIP
LIBRARY OF CONGRESS CATALOGING IN PUBLICATION DATA

Wolhart, Dayna.
Emergency vehicles / by Dayna Wolhart.
p. cm. – (Cruisin')
Summary: Discusses cars, trucks, boats, and aircraft used by fire fighters, police, Coast Guard, and others who help save lives.

ISBN 1-56065-079-6:
1. Emergency vehicles – Juvenile literature. [1. Emergency vehicles.]
I. Title. II. Series.
TL235.8.W65   1989
629.04 – dc20   89-25231
                                                              CIP
                                                              AC

PHOTO CREDITS

All American Towing: 23, 25
Deere & Company: 28
Gold Cross: 4, 9
Mayo Clinic: 30, 32
U.S. Coast Guard: 37, 38, 39, 40, 41

CAPSTONE PRESS
Box 669, Mankato, MN 56001

2

01-307

Contents

To The Rescue!

Accidents and **disasters**. Sometimes they seem too awful to think about. No matter how careful people are, accidents happen. It is good to know that there are trained people to come to the rescue. In an emergency, fire fighters, police officers, the Coast Guard and many others help save lives. Their cars, trucks, boats or aircrafts carry them to where they are needed. These vehicles carry a lot of equipment to help the rescuers do their jobs.

Right of Way

When an emergency vehicle has its sirens screaming and lights flashing, it has the **right of way**. That means the other cars and trucks on the road have to get out of the way. They must let the emergency vehicle pass them. When someone's life is in danger, right of way is important. It lets the emergency vehicle get to the emergency faster. The sooner help arrives, the better the chance of saving lives. Medical experts talk about the "golden hour" after a person has been hurt. It means the first hour. If a person gets the right care in the first hour after being hurt, there is a much better chance of getting better. That's why emergency vehicles need to go fast.

In this book, we will talk about many kinds of emergency vehicles. You will learn who uses them, and how. We will take a look "behind the scenes" to find out what makes emergency vehicles special.

Emergency Vehicle Engines

The engines of emergency vehicles work very hard. They need to go fast. They run for many hours. So some of their engine systems need to be made stronger than on regular cars and trucks. Most car or truck engines have four or six cylinders. Many emergency vehicles have eight cylinders. The more cylinders, the more power. Running engines get very hot. So they have cooling systems to take away the heat. More miles and more speed mean more heat. So many emergency vehicles have extra cooling systems. The battery is part of the car or truck's electrical system. Almost all cars and trucks have one battery. Emergency vehicles need extra electricity for their radios, sirens and flashing lights. So they often have a second battery. Some emergency vehicles are made by taking a regular car or truck **chassis**, then adding special parts. Chassis means the frame of a car or truck.

Emergency vehicles need special care. They

drive farther, and often faster, than other cars and trucks. So they need good **maintenance**. That means checking all the systems. It means changing parts that are worn out, and making sure everything works just right. Good maintenance makes the vehicles safer. It makes them more reliable.

Ambulances

What Do Ambulances Do?

Ambulances help save lives. They give medical care to people who are suddenly very sick or hurt. Most of the people who work on an ambulance are Emergency Medical Technicians, or EMTs. They are the ambulance crew. A crew is a group of people trained to work together. First the ambulance crew will decide what is wrong with the patient. They then **stabilize** the patient, or make sure that it is safe to move him or her. This might mean putting a splint on a broken leg. Or they might stop the bleeding from a bad cut. Or they might give oxygen (air) to a person who cannot breathe. Once it is safe to move the patient, the ambulance takes the patient to the hospital.

Ambulances carry many kinds of medical equipment. Oxygen bottles and resuscitators can force air into the lungs of a person who stops breathing. Back boards and cervical (neck) collars and splints help keep body parts still, in case of broken bones. Saline (salt water) solution and sterile water are to rinse wounds and burns. Bandages cover cuts and help stop bleeding. Some ambulances also carry more advanced equipment like heart monitors and machines to give electrical shocks to hearts that stop. (Sometimes giving a shock will start the heart beating again.)

The radio in an ambulance is very important. It can be moved out of the truck to where the patient is. The crew uses the radio to talk to doctors and nurses at the hospital. They tell the crew what to do for a patient. Some ambulances have cellular phones instead of radios.

Three Kinds of Ambulances

Ambulances are not all made the same way. They don't all look the same, either. Some are made in two parts. The first part is the chassis. It can be either a pickup truck chassis or a van chassis. These are made by companies that make regular trucks and vans. Then the back part is added. The back part is called a **modular box**. It has all the medical equipment in it. It makes the truck or van chassis into an ambulance. When a pickup truck is made into an ambulance, it is called Type I. A van with a modular box on the back is called Type III, or cutaway. Type II is simply a van with a higher roof. It does not hold as many patients, but it costs less. Types I and III cost about $58,000 to $65,000. Type II costs about $39,000.

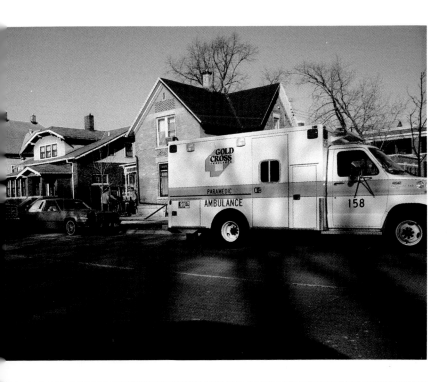

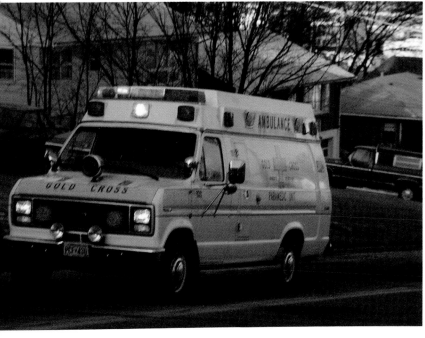

What Makes a Good Ambulance

An ambulance must be strong, but it cannot be too heavy. It must be easy to handle under very tough driving conditions. Its engine must stand up to a lot of miles. Good ambulance drivers are important. Ambulances must be easy for other drivers to hear and see. So their sirens are very loud. The trucks are often painted in bright colors, like white with red, blue or orange. They have flashing lights on top. Some trucks have the word AMBULANCE printed backwards on the front. Why backwards? That way a driver can read the word in his rear-view mirror if the ambulance comes up behind him.

Fire Trucks

Fire fighters do more than put out fires. They answer many kinds of emergency calls. That's why in cities, there are many fire stations. You may find one in every neighborhood. When an emergency happens, the fire fighters are called first. Many fire fighters are trained as EMTs, like the ambulance crews. They can give first aid while an ambulance is on its way.

Besides putting out fires, fire fighters might help clean up a chemical spill. Or they might rescue someone who was trapped in a crashed car. Like an ambulance crew, fire fighters can give

CPR. That means saving the life of a person who has stopped breathing and has no heartbeat. CPR stands for **Cardio Pulmonary Resuscitation**. That means pressing hard on a person's chest to get the heart pumping again. It also means puffing air into their mouth and lungs to get them to breathe again.

Yes, fire fighters can do all of these things. But the fire trucks are designed mainly to put out fires. Each truck has a purpose. There are three main kinds.

Pumpers

Pumpers are the trucks that get the water into the hoses and onto the fire. If the fire is in a city building, the water will come from a fire hydrant. But water does not spray out of the hydrant hard enough. So the pumps suck the water out and raise the water pressure. Then the water sprays out the hose nozzles very fast. Fire fighters measure how strong a pump is by how many **gpm** it pumps. That means gallons per minute. The biggest fire pumps can move more than 500 gpm. That is a lot! Your kitchen faucet can only pump about two or three gpm.

If the fire is in the country, there may be no hydrants. So pumpers have to get water from other places. Pumpers have huge water tanks in back. They carry enough water to put out smaller fires. When the water in the tank is not enough,

pumpers can pull water from other places. They may pump water from rivers, the ocean, lakes, even swimming pools!

Aerial Ladders

Aerial ladder trucks are the ones with the long ladders that reach way up high. Aerial means "in the air." Aerial ladder trucks help fight fires in tall buildings. The ladders come in many different lengths. The tallest ones can reach as high as 100, 150, even 200 feet. Some ladder trucks are so long they can't turn corners very well. So they have an extra steering wheel in back. This is called a tiller.

The trucks have motors that move the ladders. The ladders move three ways, They stretch out and get longer, or extend. They go up and down from the truck, or hoist and lower. They turn, or rotate, on a base on the truck. This way the fire fighters can reach many different places with the ladders. The fire fighters need to carry hoses and equipment up the ladders. There might be as many as twelve people on a ladder at one time! So the ladders must be very strong. But they must also be light. If the ladders were too heavy, the trucks would not be able to go fast enough. The ladders are made of aluminum or steel.

Elevated Platform trucks

These trucks are also made to fight fires in tall buildings. They have a bucket-like cage on the end of a long pole. It goes up and down. Some of the

poles can bend in the middle to go sideways, too. The elevated platform helps rescue people. How? Sometimes fires spread very fast. People might not be able to get out. Or the building might be so smokey they could not see. If this happens in a tall building, the fire fighters send up the elevated platform. People can climb out the windows or off the roof of the building. Then the platform lowers them safely to the ground.

The platform also takes up fire fighters and equipment. That is easier than climbing the ladder. The elevated platform's pole has a water pipe in it, too. The pipe carries up water to spray on the fire.

Ladder and platform trucks must be made steady at the bottom. Large blocks are set in front and back of the wheels. This stops the truck from rolling. Jacks brace the frame of the truck to the ground.

Making Fire Trucks

Some companies build fire trucks from start to finish. Sometimes they buy the engines from a truck maker, but they make the frame and the body and add all the equipment. Other companies buy the truck chassis and turn it into a fire vehicle. Fire trucks are expensive! Most of them cost more than a house. Some cost as much as one-half million dollars. But they last about 20 years.

Squad Cars

Squad cars are marked in a special way so everyone can tell they are police cars. Most squad cars are painted in a light color and a dark color. A shield may be painted on the door with the word POLICE. Flashing lights are mounted on a bar on top of the car.

The squad car's radio is very important. It lets the officers talk to the police station and get messages back. Through the radio, the officers learn who needs them, and where. Talking back and forth is called **communications**. Some police cars have computers in them. A computer is part of the communications system. The police use it to get facts. With their car's computer, they can check a license number. They can see if a person has a criminal record. They can learn if a car is stolen. If a car has a computer, the car needs two radios. The computer uses one radio to send and receive data, or facts. The other radio is for talking.

Sometimes when criminals are being taken to the police station, they try to hurt the officers. So squad cars have a screen between the front and back seats. The screen is made of wire or plexiglass. Plexiglass is a tough, clear plastic. It keeps the officers safe from the people they have arrested.

What Makes A Good Squad Car?

Squad cars must be safe. They must run well in all kinds of weather. They must run well on smooth roads and bumpy roads. So most squad cars have heavy duty tires that last longer and grip the road better. Squad cars must be able to go fast. They must be able to idle or stand still with their motors running, for a long time. A squad car's siren must be loud. People must be able to hear it so they can get out of the way when the police are coming.

When Are Squad Cars Used?

In big cities, squad cars are on the road almost 24 hours a day. If you call for the police, a squad car will come. Officers in squad cars do all kinds of things. They bring home lost children. They come to traffic accidents. They stop cars that are driving unsafe. They arrest criminals. They save lives.

Other Kinds of Police Cars

Not all police cars are squad cars. Squad cars are called "marked" cars. Some police cars are "unmarked." That means they look just like regular cars. Unmarked cars are not used the same way as squad cars. Unmarked cars may be used to watch people that the police think will break the law. Watching people is called **surveillance**. Unmarked cars may be used by officers who ask questions to learn all there is to know about a crime. That is called **investigating**. Also, unmarked cars may

be used by **undercover** police. That means they act like they are not police officers. They try to catch people who break the law.

Tow Trucks

Not all people think of tow trucks as emergency vehicles. They do not have sirens. They do not save people's lives the way fire trucks or ambulances do. Tow trucks can rescue cars.

The tow truck and its driver can start cars. They use cables and a motor called a **generator**. A generator makes an electric charge to take the place of the worn down battery. Using cables and a power source to start a car is called a **jump start**.

Kinds of Tow Trucks

There are two main kinds of tow trucks, **wreckers and rollbacks**. Tow trucks came to be called wreckers because some of the cars they move have been damaged or wrecked. Rollbacks are a newer kind of truck that does almost the same thing as wreckers. They just work in a different way. Rollbacks are named for the way that they tow the car.

Wreckers work by lifting the car's front wheels off the ground. A tow bar fits under the car's bumper. A machine called a winch lifts the tow bar and the front end of the car. Rollbacks have a flatbed that rolls back to the car. The car is pulled

or driven onto the flatbed. Then the flatbed rolls back up, and the car rides on the flatbed. Rollbacks work better than wreckers on newer cars. Cars used to be made all of metal. Now many car parts are plastic. The tow bar on a wrecker can damage a car's plastic bumper. Rollbacks do not.

The smallest wreckers weigh one ton. They are about the size of a pickup truck. They tow cars, vans and small trucks. There are also huge wreckers that tow semitrailer trucks. These can weigh as much as 25 tons. Rollbacks are usually one to five tons. But they may weigh up to 25 tons.

Who Uses Tow Trucks?

Many companies use tow trucks. A towing company will have a **fleet**, or group, of trucks. Car owners may call a towing company to move a car that needs to be fixed. Sometimes people park where they should not. Then someone else who needs to have the car moved might call the towing company. Towing companies stay very busy. Their trucks may work 24 hours a day. Service stations use tow trucks, too. They can tow cars to their station and do the repairs.

What Makes a Good Tow Truck ?

Tow trucks must do their job quickly, neatly and safely. If a car or truck is wrecked on a busy road, it must be moved fast. Most tow trucks carry shovels, brooms and buckets. The driver sweeps up broken glass. Many tow trucks have lights on top that flash. They warn other drivers.

A good tow truck needs a two-way radio. When a truck is out working, the company can call the driver. The driver will learn where to go next. If drivers need extra help, they can radio for help.

Tow trucks must be strong. They must last a long time. Companies that build the trucks are always trying to make their trucks better. Their engineers design new ways to get the job done. Tow trucks work hard. They have a lot of heavy equipment on them. That makes them expensive. The one-ton wreckers and rollbacks cost about $30,000 to $35,000. The big, 25-ton wreckers can cost up to one million dollars.

Snowplows

How Snowplows Work

Snowplows remove snow from roads and parking lots. Some snowplows are tractors with big buckets on the front. The bucket scoops up the snow and dumps it on a pile or in the back of a dump truck. The truck hauls the snow away.

Some pickup trucks, dump trucks and road graders have blades on them. As the truck drives, the blade pushes the snow in front of it, or to the left or right. A V-plow has a big wedge in front. It pushes the snow left and right at the same time.

Some snowplows are really huge snow throwers. They have spinning blades that cut into the snow and throws it to the side. Some plows are also sanders. They have a big dumper on the back. They spread sand and salt or other chemicals on the road. That fights ice after the plow goes through.

Snowplow Safety

Snowplows almost always work in bad weather. During a storm, it's very hard to see. And the plowing or snow throwing kicks up even more snow. So snowplows have flashing lights on them to warn other drivers. It is also hard for the plow driver to see the road. So the truck or tractor must let the driver see over the hood. Good heaters inside the truck keep ice off the windows.

Snowplows have two-way radios in them, and special controls to make the plow go up and down. The truck frames have to be extra strong, and their engines must be powerful. That way they can carry the extra weight of the plow, the snow and the sand.

Rescue Aircraft

Airplanes and helicopters can be used as emergency vehicles. Sometimes they are used for a search and rescue, or SAR missions. SAR is done by groups like the Civil Air Patrol, units of the Armed Forces, police departments, and others. They may search for planes that crash.

But search and rescue are not the only jobs for emergency aircraft. Sometimes bad weather or accidents wipe out roads, homes and telephone lines. Floods, tornadoes, earthquakes, forest fires, hurricanes or chemical spills are called *disasters.* A disaster is when something happens that destroys property and sometimes people. When disasters happen, planes and helicopters often help bring in food, clothes and medicine to people who need them. This is called disaster relief. Sometimes they fly people out of the disaster area. When all the people are taken away from a dangerous place, it is called **evacuation**.

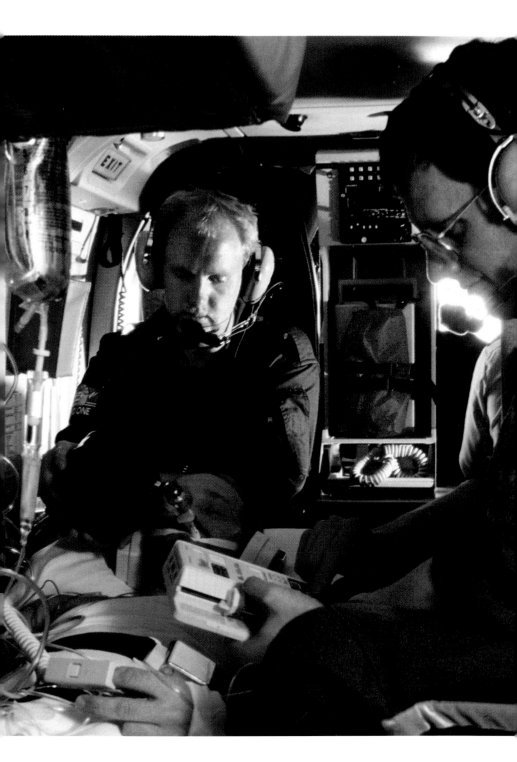

Flying Ambulances

Planes and helicopters also move sick and hurt people to hospitals. They are used when the patient has a very long way to travel. Or they are used when a regular ambulance could not get through. Or they are used when a regular ambulance would be too slow. Some big cities have very bad traffic jams. Ambulance trucks cannot drive fast on a highway that is blocked by other cars. Then helicopters are much faster. They can fly over the traffic jam. Some small towns don't have hospitals. Or small hospitals may not have the right equipment to treat a person who is very sick. If a very sick person needs to go to a far away hospital, he or she will go by plane or helicopter.

Most helicopters can only fly about 150 to 200 miles in one trip. So they are used more in cities. If the hospital is more than 200 miles away, a plane will be used. Ambulance airplanes are often small jets, turbo-props and twin engine prop planes. Medical supplies and equipment are added. Medical helicopters often have twin engines, too. Having two engines makes them safer, in case one engine stops working in the middle of a flight. Medical aircraft have on board the kind of medical equipment you would find in an ambulance truck. Some even have very advanced equipment, like what you would find in a hospital emergency room.

Medical aircraft cost a lot of money. They can cost up to 2 million dollars or more. It depends on the size of the aircraft and the kind of medical equipment carried on the aircraft. The high cost is why many hospitals do not buy their own aircraft. Some rent helicopters, and pilots to fly them. Then the hospital puts its own medical crew on the helicopter. Some hospitals hire air ambulance companies to move their patients. These companies have their own medical crews on the aircraft.

Radio Systems

Most medical aircraft have two radio systems. One system is for the pilot. It is called the aviation radio. The pilot needs the radio to talk to the flight control towers. In an emergency, the flight control towers give the medical aircraft right of way. The second radio system is for the medical crew. The medical radios are made with computers in them, to dial in many channels, or **frequencies**. That's because the medical team needs to talk to many different people on the ground. They talk to doctors and nurses at hospitals. They may need to talk to the police and fire departments. That's because helicopters often have to land in places besides airports. So the police and fire departments have to clear a landing zone. The medical team often has to bring together many groups of people. They may talk to forest rangers, or ski patrols, or small airports. So their radios can work on thousands of frequencies. That is a lot! The radios in most other emergency vehicles only work on about two to ten frequencies.

Emergency Boats

Emergency boats patrol in ocean waters and on rivers and lakes. Rivers and lakes which are inside the borders of our country are called **inland waters**. Ocean-going and inland water emergency boats can do many different jobs.

The boats are like police cars when they direct traffic or stop people from breaking the law. In the ocean, the U.S. Coast Guard stops people who try to bring drugs into our country. Inland water patrol boats stop people who are using boats unsafely. The Coast Guard and inland water patrols help other boats by putting out **buoys**. Buoys are like floating road signs.

Sometimes boats at sea or on a lake catch fire. Emergency boats help put the fires out. They have pumps and hoses on board to suck up water and spray it on a burning boat. Sometimes dangerous chemicals, like oil, are spilled on or in the water. Then emergency boats work to keep people away from the danger. They also help in cleaning up the mess.

Sometimes boats out on the water run into trouble. A boat's engine might stop. A person might fall overboard. Or the boat might start to sink. Sometimes planes crash on the water. When any of these things happen, the people need to be saved. When a boat or plane is in trouble, the crew sends out a **distress signal**. That means they use their radio to say they need help. If a boat does not have a radio, the crew might use flashing lights or send up flares or start a small fire. These are all signs of distress, or trouble.

SAR on the Water

When a boat or plane over water sends a distress signal, the Coast Guard or inland water patrol goes into action. They rescue people from the boat or crashed plane. They look for people who might have fallen into the water. They tow damaged boats to shore. Most rivers and lakes are small enough that boats in distress are not too hard to find. But at sea, finding a boat can be much harder. That's because a boat in the water does not stay in one place. Wind and waves make it drift. To do search and rescue, the Coast Guard or water patrol must look at the wind's speed and direction. They think about water currents and tides. They figure out where the boat might be. They plot a course and a search pattern. Then all the SAR vehicles go into action.

Of course, boats are a big part of SAR on the water. But planes and helicopters are also used. The Coast Guard has its own aircraft. But most

inland water patrols do not. They would be more likely to work with the Civil Air Patrol or the local police if they needed aircraft for SAR.

Coast Guard Ships and Boats

The Coast Guard patrols the largest waters of the United States. Search and rescue missions are one of the main things the Coast Guard does. The Coast Guard has hundreds of boats and ships. There are many different kinds, sizes and shapes. They do different jobs. We will talk about some of the boats that would be used in emergencies.

The largest ships are called **cutters**. They range in size from 210 feet long to 378 feet long. These big ships are made to go far out to sea. They are often away for a long, long time. So they have space for the crew to eat and sleep. Cutters also have big 5-inch wide guns and machine guns on them. All Coast Guard vessels are armed with at least small guns like pistols. Cutters are big enough to carry helicopters and even smaller boats to help with rescues. If the cutter itself started to sink, it has lifeboats to save the crew.

Patrol boats and tugs are strong. They work well in all kinds of weather for rescue and towing. Their sizes range from 82 feet to 213 feet. Motor lifeboats are very special rescue boats. They can save people and boats even in the worst weather. They are almost unsinkable! Motor lifeboats are

self-bailing. That means that if water gets into the boat, the boat can get rid of it. Motor lifeboats are **self-righting**, too. That means that if the boat tips over in the water, it can turn itself upright again. Most motor lifeboats are 44 feet long. They do not stay out to sea for a long time. Most of them stay at rescue stations and go out when they are needed.

The Coast Guard's ships and boats are made especially for the Coast Guard. The boats come in three different colors – red, white and black. The name COAST GUARD and their emblem is always in plain view. The boats and ships that do rescues are designed to go fast. They are **maneuverable**. That means they can start, stop and turn quickly. The boats have aluminum, steel or fiberglass **hulls**. The hull is the boat's outside walls. Most of the engines burn diesel fuel. All of the boats carry first aid kits. If someone they rescue is hurt, the crew can give help while they are on the way to shore. Like other emergency vehicles, Coast Guard boats have good communications systems. If a ship at sea runs into trouble, it can call the Coast Guard's Rescue Coordination Center. Coordination means making sure all parts work together. The Rescue Coordination Center sends boats and aircraft to the ship in distress. With radios, telegraphs, and telephones, every Coast Guard ship and aircraft stays in touch with its base. They also talk to other ships. That way they can all work together.

Inland Water Patrol Boats

Inland water patrol boats are smaller than most Coast Guard boats. But their jobs are much the same as the Coast Guard's – safety, rescue and law enforcement. The inland boats range in size from 16 feet to 22 feet. Many water patrols also use inflatable rubber rafts that are nine feet or 16 feet long. The rafts are for dive teams. Dive teams wear wetsuits, masks and air tanks. They can go under the water to look for people.

The equipment on the bigger boats includes pumps that can suck up water to spray on a burning boat. The pumps also can be used to pump air into a sinking boat to keep it floating long enough to tow it to shore. The boats carry ropes, life rings and long poles. They can be used to pull someone out of the water. Rescue boats in cold places carry cold water rescue suits. They protect the rescuers from freezing to death if they have to jump in the water to save someone. All the boats carry first aid kits. And of course, they all have communications equipment. Like police cars, some of the boats have computers for catching criminals.

Water patrol boats must be good work boats. They must be big enough to hold patrol officers, equipment and people who have been rescued. But they must be able to go fast when they are on their way to a rescue. Water patrol boats have heavy duty engines. The boats that become patrol boats are chosen because they will handle well in rough water. These boats are not designed to be only water patrol boats. The water patrol departments buy regular boats and add equipment to meet their needs. The departments add flashing lights and sirens. They add extra bright side lights to see at night. Then they paint the boats to show that they are patrol boats.

To Learn More

You have just read a little about some kinds of emergency vehicles. There is so much more you can learn! If you are interested in learning more about emergencies and rescues, visit your library. Most libraries have lots of films and videotapes. They would show emergency vehicles in action.

Another way is to visit and talk to the emergency crews when they are not in the middle of a rescue. The men and women who work on emergency vehicles like to help people. If you set it up in advance, they would welcome a visit. You could go with your school class, church group or your scout troop. Your local police, fire department, hospital, department of transportation or Coast Guard can teach you a lot about emergencies and rescues as well as safety.

Glossary

Aerial Ladder — A special ladder on a fire truck that can reach as high as 200 feet in the air.

Buoys — Guides, like floating road signs, put in the water by the Coast Guard to help other boats.

(CPR) Cardio Pulmonary Resuscitation — Saving the life of a person who has stopped breathing and has no heart beat by pushing on their chest and forcing air into their lungs.

Chassis — The frame of a vehicle, it is what the body sits on.

Communications — Police officers talking to a person at the police station over a two-way radio.

Cutters — Large ships that can carry helicopters and smaller boats to the scene of a rescue.

Disasters — Bad weather or an accident that destroys property and sometimes people.

Distress Signals — A boat may call for help by using its radio, sending up flares or starting a small fire.

Evacuation — When all people are taken away from a dangerous area.

Fleet — A group of several tow trucks belonging to one company.

Frequencies — Different channels that radios can broadcast on.

GPM (Gallons Per Minute) — The number of gallons a fire truck can pump in one minute. Some trucks can pump 500 gallons in one minute.

Generator — A special motor used by a tow truck driver to help start a car whose battery has worn down.

Hulls — The outside walls of a boat. They are made of aluminum, steel or fiberglass.

Inland Waters — Rivers and lakes inside the borders of our country.

Investigating — Asking questions and learning all there is to know about a crime.

Jump Start — To start a car whose battery has worn down by using cables and a generator.

Maintenance — Checking all systems of a vehicle to make sure everything works just right.

Maneuverable — Being able to start, stop and turn easily.

Modular Box — The box on the back of an ambulance that holds all the medical equipment.

Right of Way — All cars and trucks must pull over to the side of the road when they hear an emergency vehicle's siren.

Rollbacks — A newer type of tow truck that carries the damaged car on a flatbed.

Self-bailing — A boat that automatically gets water out of its hull if too much water is in the boat.

Self-righting — A motor lifeboat that can turn itself right side up if it tips over in the water.

Squad Car — A police car that is marked with special colors and POLICE written on the doors.

Stabilize — To make sure it is safe to move an injured or sick person.

Surveillance — Watching people who the police believe might break the law.

Undercover — Officers who act like they are not police officers to try to catch criminals.

Wreckers — A tow truck that moves cars that are damaged or wrecked.